COOL CAREERS WITHOUT COLLEGE
FOR PEOPLE WHO LOVE
READING AND RESEARCH

JANELLE ASSELIN AND REBECCA T. KLEIN

Rosen
YA™

New York

Published in 2018 by The Rosen Publishing Group, Inc.
29 East 21st Street, New York, NY 10010

Library of Congress Cataloging-in-Publication Data

Names: Asselin, Janelle, author. | Klein, Rebecca T., author.
Title: Cool careers without college for people who love reading and research / Janelle Asselin and Rebecca T. Klein.
Description: First edition. | New York : Rosen Publishing, 2018 | Series: Cool careers without college | Includes bibliographical references and index.
Identifiers: ISBN 9781508175421 (library bound)
Subjects: LCSH: Book industries and trade—Vocational guidance—Juvenile literature. | Information science—Vocational guidance—Juvenile literature. | Library science—Vocational guidance—Juvenile literature. | Authorship—Vocational guidance—Juvenile literature. | Research—Vocational guidance—Juvenile literature. | Blogs—Vocational guidance—Juvenile literature.
Classification: LCC Z471.A87 2018 | DDC 028.1023—dc23

Manufactured in China

CONTENTS

INTRODUCTION

One of the most common misconceptions about careers today is that you must have a college degree in order to have a worthwhile job. The truth is that there are a lot of options for people who would rather save the cost of college and get right to work. College costs have risen over 1,120 percent in the last thirty years, making it unaffordable for many people. But for those who enjoy reading and research, it could seem like the options out there are limited. After all, those are interests that are often linked closely with being a student. Thankfully, there are several possibilities for readers and researchers and they don't all involve college.

There are many alternatives to college out there, and the easiest one is to go straight into working in a field

Your love for reading and research can lead you straight into several careers that do not require college, including writing, genealogy, library work, and legal research.

you're passionate about already. There are job opportunities in areas like writing, owning or managing a bookstore, working in a library, doing genealogical research, selling antiques, and assisting lawyers. While some of these positions may encourage some sort of certificate program, the majority of them require nothing more than a passion for reading and research.

The greatest asset to those who are looking to develop a career without a college degree is experience, so finding a career path you enjoy and will work in for a while is important. A lot of the jobs listed in the following sections are entry-level positions, but there's career growth available for those who want it. Particularly for journalists and writers, the growth potential is limitless with the right combination of determination and skill.

Still, as fans of reading and research are well aware, it doesn't hurt to investigate all the options thoroughly. This book can be a great help in determining what kind of career to have, as can many of the websites and books we recommend. When building a career in any of the areas we've suggested, having a thorough understanding of what the job entails can really help give a candidate an advantage over the competition. Read as many books and websites on relevant topics as possible and stay up-to-date on relevant current events. This can mean being aware of current trends in fiction or the newest Supreme Court cases, depending on the career involved. People who already love reading and research should have no problem with staying on top of important topics.

The first step in having a successful career without spending tens—or maybe even hundreds—of thousands of dollars on college is right here in this book. The next step is to decide what career path to start on and then get moving.

CHAPTER 1

TELLING IT LIKE IT IS: A CAREER AS A JOURNALIST

Starting a career as a journalist can be incredibly challenging, but offers a great deal of growth potential. There are many opportunities for aspiring journalists to get involved in their communities or particular areas of interest, which makes it easier to break into than a lot of other careers. Plus, journalism is something one can get into a little at a time, meaning a journalist can work another job to pay

Breaking into a career in journalism requires patience and tenacity, but it can be very rewarding and can take you to all kinds of new and interesting locations!

the bills while trying to break in. At the same time, being a journalist requires solid writing skills and knowledge of journalistic ethics, among other things.

PREPARING YOURSELF

The first step to being a journalist is to do some research. The first thing to research is how to be a journalist. Check out any number of books on the topic of being a journalist and learn about the best ways to go about writing on different topics. For instance, a different approach and code of behavior is required when writing about sexual harassment versus writing about the local cat show. Both will require the basics of being a journalist, but the writer may need to approach each very differently. That's not where the reading and research ends, though.

Think about something that you're particularly interested in—guess what? There are journalists who write about that topic. Whether you're interested in animals, celebrities, farming, architecture, books, food, your city, or something else, the chances are very good that there are news outlets that cover that topic. This could mean blogs, news websites, newspapers, magazines, and other forms of news outlets. There are many different kinds of journalists with a lot of different kinds of jobs. Of course, that doesn't always mean it's easy to get a job. In reality, it can be challenging to break in as a journalist, but here are a few quick tips.

First, know the topic you want to write about above all else. If you're passionate about a topic, it will only help your writing. This is where reading and research come into play. Maybe you think that architecture is really interesting, but you don't know a lot about it yet. Study architecture books, read architecture websites, go on architectural tours, and do whatever possible to learn more about the topic. It's also particularly helpful to attend local events so as to make contacts that can help with getting writing assignments. Maybe that's the editor of the local paper, or maybe it's a local blog that wants someone to cover news occasionally. It doesn't mean this is the only topic that a journalist will ever cover, but having a particular point of interest helps one break in. Journalist Sarah Jaffe, author of

Reporter Sanaa Hammoud works for the Al Jazeera network. Here, she interviews former US President Jimmy Carter at a Democratic National Convention.

Necessary Trouble, started her journalism career by writing about comic books and evolved it into writing about politics and labor. Occasionally she still writes about comic books, but her career has taken her other places now. It's good to have a starting point, but not be locked into that.

Second, know that in order to break in as a paid journalist, some unpaid work may be necessary to start. Beware of being taken advantage of, though. Starting a blog is a great way to get exposure as an expert on a topic and is something you can own. Working for someone who is making money but can't pay you, however, can be a challenging experience. Weigh the pros and cons of any free work you may do. Not everyone is looking out for their writers' best interests. Still, working for exposure can be a good way to break in and make a name for yourself on a particular topic.

Third, embrace social media. Most journalists today have a strong social media presence, particularly on sites like Twitter and Instagram. This is another good way to break in, too. It may be unpaid work, but it can establish a strong writer with a particular niche very well. For instance, a young writer with an interest in the Black Lives Matter movement might attend some rallies and events and livetweet the proceedings. This could lead to the writer getting cited as a source by other journalists or asked to write about the experience for a news outlet. Plus, then the writer can point to the tweets in question while pitching to various outlets about the experience.

Fourth, keep pitching and don't let rejection get you down. Researching the right people to pitch to can be exhausting, but it's important to make contacts and pitch stories. That's how journalists get paid. If you've established yourself a bit, you can point to writing samples, but if you're still breaking in, be prepared to work hard while pitching. Research every single outlet that's of interest and know what they cover, how they cover it, and who the key players are. If you're a queer woman who wants to write for Autostraddle, who might be a good person to talk to? That all depends on the topic, but can easily be researched on Autostraddle's Meet the Team page. Remember that rejection is all part of the process of being a journalist or writer of any type (more on that in a bit), so to try to not take it personally. There's no magic number of rejections before you start getting published and no magic way to feel okay about getting rejected when pitches you care about aren't selected. But good journalists know to persevere even when stories they care about aren't accepted anywhere. Sometimes that means the right home hasn't been found for a piece yet, and sometimes it means the journalist needs to make a home for it themselves.

CAREER POTENTIAL

The nice thing about being a journalist is that there's unlimited potential to turn it into any kind of career you want. If you want to be a staff writer somewhere, there's a chance to

With constant increases in available technology, the public appetite for news media continues to grow. This growth creates more and more opportunities for various types of journalism careers.

do that at many websites and newspapers around the world. If you'd prefer to be freelance and write for many different websites on the same topic, that's possible, too. Even as print newspapers struggle and websites may not always be making the most money, the world needs journalists. Plus, the opportunities for journalists don't begin and end at the written word. There is room for those who make a name for themselves to break into video reporting, producing, editing, and other directions. The next wave of journalists may even end up working in all-new ways that we haven't thought of yet, so it's also important to remain flexible and open to new ways of reporting news.

That being said, in the last decade or so the landscape of the world of journalism has shifted dramatically, and the field has slowly stopped growing in the way it was. While staff positions used to be the norm, today many journalists are freelancers, making ends meet by putting together multiple projects and assignments every month. On the one hand, this has relaxed the field of journalism, and has led to requirements for becoming a journalist to be more lax, allowing those without degrees to make successful careers. On the other hand, it leaves an uncertain path for those who want to be journalists today.

FOR MORE INFORMATION

ORGANIZATIONS

American Press Institute
4401 Wilson Boulevard, Suite 900
Arlington, VA 22203
(571) 366-1200
Website: http://www.americanpressinstitute.org
The American Press Institute is an educational
   non-profit organization that conducts research and
   training for reporters and journalistic educators.

Canadian Association of Journalists
P.O. Box 117, Station F
Toronto, ON M4Y 2L4
Website: http://www.caj.ca
From University classrooms to the national Canadian
   stage, CAJ works to promote journalistic excellence.
   The organization stages conferences and workshops,
   and connects journalists across the country through
   its list serves.

Journalism Education Association
828 Mid-Campus Drive South
Manhattan, KS 66506-1505

(866) 532-5532
Website: http://jea.org
The Journalism Education Association is the largest
    scholastic journalism organization for teachers
    and advisers.

National Association of Black Journalists
1100 Knight Hall, Suite 3100
College Park, MD 20742
(301) 405-0248
Website: http://www.nabj.org/
The National Association of Black Journalists (NABJ) is
    an organization of journalists, students and media-
    related professionals that provides quality programs
    and services to and advocates on behalf of black
    journalists worldwide.

Society of Professional Journalists
Eugene S. Pulliam National Journalism Center
3909 N. Meridian St., Indianapolis, IN 46208
(317) 927-8000
Website: http://www.spj.org
The Society of Professional Journalists strives to protect
    First Amendment rights and Freedom of Information.

Through grassroots activism, SPJ confronts all of the issues facing modern journalists.

BOOKS

Ekanem, Anthony. *Career in Journalism: A Beginner's Guide to Becoming a Journalist.* CreateSpace Independent Publishing, 2016.

Fromm, Megan. *Accuracy in Media.* New York, NY: Rosen Publishing, 2015.

Hall, Homer. *Student Journalism and Media Literacy.* New York, NY: Rosen Publishing, 2015.

WEBSITES

Because of the changing nature of internet links, Rosen Publishing has developed an online list of websites related to the subject of this book. This site is updated regularly. Please use this link to access the list:

http://www.rosenlinks.com/CCWC/reading

CHAPTER 2

AMAZING STORIES: A CAREER AS A FICTION WRITER

For someone who loves reading and research an obvious career choice is to become a writer. We've already covered one type of writer—the journalist—but there are a lot of other kinds of writers. Deciding where to focus and how to approach your career can seem overwhelming when you're considering the career of a writer, but the good news is that there are many great options and directions in which you can go. A popular career option for writers is that of being a fiction writer.

Toni Morrison has established a career as one of the most respected and beloved fiction writers of our time. She has received the Pulitzer Prize, the American Book Award, and the Nobel Prize for Literature, among other awards and accolades.

PREPARING YOURSELF

Just like with beginning a career in journalism, the way to start as a fiction writer is to focus on what you already love. Sci-fi or fantasy fans may be best off considering a career as a sci-fi or fantasy writer. Readers who adore historical research and nonfiction would do well to consider writing their own nonfiction book. One key point to being a writer: once you've started writing, you're a writer. Getting published and paid is important, especially if you're building a career, but there is no need to refer to yourself as an aspiring writer if you're actively writing. "Aspiring writers" are writers. Study

The most essential part of being a writer is to actually do the work of writing. It can be difficult to get started, but you don't have to be intimidated. Getting those words down is the first step toward a writing career.

COMIC BOOK WRITER

Being a comic book writer can involve writing either fiction or nonfiction, but either way it's a different beast than writing prose. There are major format and medium differences. Anyone who is an aspiring comics writer should spend a lot of time reading all sorts of comic books, including graphic novels, autobiographical comics, small press comics, and mainstream comics. The main difference between writing prose and writing a comic book is that, for the most part, comic books are written in a script format rather than in prose. Plus, anyone writing comics should have some understanding of pacing and panel layouts in comics, even if you're not an artist.

When you're breaking into comics, generally you don't need an agent. An agent can be helpful if you're moving from the world of prose writing into comics writing, but most comics' publishers aren't used to working with literary agents unless it's a comics publisher that's owned by a more traditional publisher. The best way to break into comics is simply by making comics. Find an artist buddy and get your work out there. Make your own webcomic. Do what you can to get people reading what you're doing, and make contacts in the industry.

your craft and take it seriously, but above all, write. And once you're a writer, the possibilities are endless. Want to try your hand in historical fiction, but also write historical nonfiction and essays? You can build the kind of career you want. Let's explore some of the options.

When people think of "writers," they're usually thinking of fiction. If this is your chosen career path, you have to be prepared for a lot of people to minimize what you're doing until you gain success, but there's a lot of room for mid-list authors who are able to pay their bills through steady and consistent writing. Don't be discouraged by the statistics and stereotypes out there about writers. Know that hard work, determination, and, of course, well-honed talent will help you make a career. There are no guarantees that you'll become famous, of course, but many people find a niche that works well for them.

Some of the hardest-working classes of writers are romance, sci-fi, and fantasy writers.These writers have dedicated fan bases, and often (when successful), work on a series of novels. Many of of these writers put out books so regularly that their fans know to expect a book every year or two. This requires a lot of dedication from the writers involved. And you may never become a household name to anyone but a set of devoted fans. But

While some readers consume fiction voraciously through digital formats like Nook and Kindle, others prefer to read books the old fashioned way, in print. There is still a huge market for fiction!

no matter what your genre of choice is, there's often a niche for you, complete with a special kind of agent and publisher for you.

To break in as a fiction writer, usually the writer must have at least one completed manuscript that they can submit to agents for consideration. This shows that you can construct a complete and compelling narrative. Even if it's not in perfect shape, the basic bones of the story should be there so that the agents and publishers can see what kind of writer you are. It's hard to get published without an agent, so for most people they're a necessity. To find agents, books like the *Writer's Market* offer all sorts of listings. It pays to do research, though, and really understand the agents to which you're submitting. Twitter is also a surprisingly good place to find agents that might be good to speak with. It's an especially good way to see what agents might be looking for, as some even tweet about that!

When submitting a book to an agent, a writer should have at least a rudimentary book proposal. Sample proposals can be found online, but generally have to include some information about the writer, the possible audience for the book, and sample chapters. You'll want your proposal to be very polished, which may mean getting friends (who you trust to give an honest opinion) to read it over a few times.

Finally, a route that is open to writers who have a lot of hustle is the self-publishing route, especially in the age of e-books. There are many authors, again particularly in romance, and sci-fi, and fantasy, who have made names and careers for themselves simply by publishing on Amazon, working hard to get the word out about their book, and getting good reviews. There are advantages and disadvantages to this kind of publishing, but it's worth considering.

CAREER POTENTIAL

It's hard to know exact data on the future of writing, especially as so many writers are not employees of any company but rather freelancers. Still, projections have the field growing by more than 26,000 jobs between 2014 and 2024. No matter what kind of writer you want to be, the basics are the same: study your craft, read as many books about writing as possible, read everything and anything you possibly can, accept notes with good grace, and be ready to work hard. Although people often think of writing as a very romantic pursuit, the reality is that if you want to make money as a writer, you must be willing to work hard, even when it doesn't feel romantic or pleasurable. Writing can be a rewarding career, and it doesn't require any special education or certification, but it does require perseverance and commitment.

FOR MORE INFORMATION

ORGANIZATIONS

Science Fiction and Fantasy Writers Association
SFWA, Inc.
PO Box 3238
Enfield, CT 06083-3238
Website: http://www.sfwa.org
SFWA promotes, defends, supports and advocates for
   writers in the science fiction, fantasy, and related
   genres.

Society of Children's Book Writers and Illustrators
4727 Wilshire Blvd., Suite 301
Los Angeles, CA 90010
Website: http://www.scbwi.org
This organization supports the creation of literature for
   children and helps to create a community of writers
   and illustrators.

BOOKS

Burroway, Janet and Elizabeth Stucky-French. *Writing
   Fiction: A Guide to Narrative Craft*. New York, NY:
   Pearson, 2014.

Card, Orson Scott. *How to Write Science Fiction and Fantasy.* Writer's Digest Books, 2015.
Weiland, K.M. *Structuring Your Novel: Essential Keys For Writing an Outstanding Story.* PenForASword, 2013.

WEBSITES

Because of the changing nature of internet links, Rosen Publishing has developed an online list of websites related to the subject of this book. This site is updated regularly. Please use this link to access the list:

http://www.rosenlinks.com/CCWC/reading

CHAPTER 3

THE TRUTH AND NOTHING BUT THE TRUTH: A CAREER AS A NONFICTION WRITER

One of the most obvious careers one can get into as someone who loves research in particular is as a nonfiction writer. Nonfiction writers can cover a number of topics in a variety of ways, but the basic gist is that they are writing about topics that are not made up. The book you're reading right now is a nonfiction book, and the authors are nonfiction writers. The nice thing about nonfiction is that if you've worked as a journalist or have written shorter nonfiction essays, you might be hired to write nonfiction books without even submitting your own ideas. But if you have an idea that you

Laura Hillenbrand has found huge success as a nonfiction writer, receiving acclaim for her magazine articles and for her two nonfiction books, *Seabiscuit* and *Unbroken*.

think is perfect for a nonfiction book, whether it's a crafting guide or a historical analysis of women's roles in 18th century England, the process for getting published is pretty similar to the process for fiction books. It's just the subject matter that is different. Nonfiction leaves lots of room for creativity as well as analysis. There are many different styles and niches in the nonfiction genre.

ADVICE FROM LITERARY AGENT MARIA VICENTE:

What advice would you give young, aspiring writers?
To always be working on something new. Try not to follow trends and write whatever it is you're truly passionate about. Decide early on if you want to make a career out of being a writer. Do the research on different types of publishing paths and which one will work best for you, your writing style, and your goals.

What do you look for in a book proposal that makes you want to represent a writer?
Book proposals with inventive ideas always stand out – something that hasn't been done before. I want to represent writers with a unique writing style, with the drive to always keep writing, and with the ability to keep the business side of writing in mind as they make decisions.

What's the best way for a writer to find an agent? Search online for various literary agencies and agents. Pay attention to what they represent and what is on their wish lists. Learn how to write a great query letter (there are multiple resources online) and contact the agents who are the best fit for your project.

PREPARING YOURSELF

You'll want to read up on what it takes to be a nonfiction writer and maybe take a class or two on writing to help you develop your voice. It can sometimes be harder to make nonfiction as interesting as fiction, depending on the writer, so you'll want to understand how to craft a narrative around a nonfiction topic. The Media Bistro website has some online seminars that can be very helpful for this sort of thing. Keeping readers engaged is just as important to a nonfiction writer as it is to a fiction writer. And if the topic you want to write about isn't an easy one, that's even more true. Part of researching and understanding what makes a good nonfiction writer is understanding the ethics of how you write about true events, for instance, and how to properly quote interview subjects. A lot of journalism resources can also be helpful on this kind of topic.

Compiling accurate research is an essential part of writing a nonfiction book. Putting together a books proposal is also an important step in marketing your book to agents and publishers.

Similar to a fiction writer, to find an agent and attempt to get published, a nonfiction writer will want to put together a book proposal. The major difference between fiction and nonfiction book proposals, however, is that many agents and publishers don't want a nonfiction manuscript to be finished before they buy it, because they want to be able to shape the direction and style of the book in a way that is very specific to nonfiction. Plus, because a lot of nonfiction books are related to current events or follow a particular season or event, publishers will want them to be as current and fresh as possible. Your book proposal should have sample chapters and a full outline, so don't think you can get away with no writing up front. Present the most polished proposal as possible at this stage, as it is an important step to getting published.

Some writers who make a name for themselves as journalists or in other areas of writing will get commissioned to write a book on a specific topic. You can create relationships with editors at publishers you like to see if this helps you get hired to write books as well. This is where working in an area that you're particularly interested in can really help. You may be able to get hired to write a book without having to pitch one around, but keep in mind this is generally only true if you've established yourself as a writer in another arena. If you're

There are endless opportunities for nonfiction writers to cover a wealth of topics. Nonfiction books are written in various styles, from matter-of-fact journalism to creative, poetic essays.

writing about something you're really passionate about and it's not a book that you've been commissioned to write, it's important that you know your agent has the best interests of you and your project in mind. Once you have an agent, you can pinpoint the best time and place to shop your book.

Research is particularly important for nonfiction writers, and will be a key component of the work. Being comfortable with working in libraries and online will really help aspiring nonfiction writers. Again, whether you're writing a crafting book or a historical analysis, research is your friend. Take your time to know your subject well before you sit down to write.

CAREER POTENTIAL

The prospects for nonfiction writers are likely better than for fiction writers, as nonfiction makes up a larger number of books published in a given year, and trends for fiction tend to keep the number of fiction books pretty limited every year. There are still trends to follow, however, so don't think it'll be easy. Writers who are flexible and can write about a number of different topics may find it easier to break into writing nonfiction, although starting with an agent is your best option. You might choose to focus on history, creative nonfiction (essays about your experiences, thoughts, and beliefs), music reviews, or biography. Find an agent who specializes in your genre, or who at least has had some success in similar areas. Like many of the other careers mentioned in this book, nonfiction writing may not earn you a living over night, but with time and commitment, you may be able to make enough money from your writing to support yourself.

ORGANIZATIONS

American Society of Journalists and Authors
355 Lexington Avenue, 15th Floor
New York, NY 10017-6603
(212) 997-0947
Website: http://www.asja.org
This is the premiere professional organization for
   writers of all types on nonfiction.

Association of Writers & Writing Programs
George Mason University
4400 University Drive
MSN 1E3
Fairfax, VA 22030
(703) 993-4301
Website: https://www.awpwriter.org
AWP provides support, advocacy, resources, and
   community to nearly 50,000 writers, 550 college
   and university creative writing programs, and 150
   writers' conferences and centers.

International Writing Centers Association
705 Palomar Airport Road

Carlsbad, CA 92011

(760) 268-1567

Website: http://writingcenters.org

The International Writing Centers Association fosters the
development of writing center directors, tutors, and
staff by sponsoring meetings, publications, and other
professional activities; by encouraging scholarship
connected to writing center-related fields.

National Association of Memoir Writers

1700 Solano Ave

Berkeley, CA 94707, USA

(510) 859-4718

Website: http://www.namw.org

NAMW empowers memoir writers through teleseminars,
ebooks, and many other types of resources.

Nonfiction Authors Association

11230 Gold Express Dr. #310-413

Gold River, CA 95670

(877) 800-1097

Website: http://nonfictionauthorsassociation.com

This organization provides resources, support,
and education for authors of nonfiction books.

BOOKS

Boufis, Christina. *The Complete Idiot's Guide to Writing Nonfiction.* New York, NY:. ALPHA Books, 2012.

Gutkind, Lee. *You Can't Make This Stuff Up: The Complete Guide to Writing Creative Nonfiction.* Boston, MA: De Capo, 2012.

Poynter, Dan. *Writing Nonfiction: Turning Thoughts Into Books.* 6th Edition. Para Publishing, 2014.

WEBSITES

Because of the changing nature of internet links, Rosen Publishing has developed an online list of websites related to the subject of this book. This site is updated regularly. Please use this link to access the list:

http://www.rosenlinks.com/CCWC/reading

CHAPTER 4

MAY I HELP YOU? A CAREER AS A WRITER'S ASSISTANT

For many aspiring writers, the job of assisting another writer is seen as a stepping stone to paying the bills entirely with one's own writing. But for those who love administrative tasks and keeping people organized, being a writer's assistant can be a long-term career in its own right. It certainly can be rewarding in a very different way than being a writer is rewarding. There are opportunities to work with a wide range of writers, too, from those just starting out who need a little bit of help to those who need constant assistance with things like fan mail and appearance coordination. Writers often need someone to help them stay on top of social media and manage new technology.

It is a good way to learn how to be a successful writer and learn all of the things required of a successful writer, certainly. Working with someone who has an established career in the field you want to work in is a great idea— mentorship can be more valuable than any degree when you have the right mentor. Finding a writer to work with may be

Being a writer's assistant can allow you to explore the world and routines of a working writer. It might lead you to a career of your own in writing, or it might be a career within itself.

the most challenging aspect of this career, but as with most of these fields, networking can be immensely helpful. Visiting local readings and signings, attending conventions that writers attend, and generally being involved in the literary scene will introduce you to people who may need your help. The internet can also be very helpful for this sort of thing. Making connections via social media with writers can lead you to work as well.

NOTES FROM A WRITER'S ASSISTANT

Writer's assistant Kelly McDonald (her real name is being withheld for privacy) was happy to share some experiences of working for a writer.

"The surprising thing about being a writer's assistant is that it has much less to do with publishing or writing as it does administrative tasks. For example, as a highly successful writer [the person I work with] has tons of readings, performances, and so on, so a lot of my work involves coordination and documentation. Keeping track of all her performances, lectures is part of my job, along with updating her CV and helping out with reports to the university on her activities. I also track down articles and interviews about her, along with academic research on her work.

I have, on occasion, edited her work, and it really helps. I have a firm background on the genre she is working in. A lot of this has come from working with her over the years, so I have a sense of how she would want things said or what she would likely phrase something.

What she recognized about me was I'm incredibly organized. I don't require a lot of handholding and directions. So organization and research skills would be at the top, but also having a sixth sense! It's exciting if you are into research because she'll throw me a curveball for something she's writing and needs researched."

PREPARING YOURSELF

If you love reading and research, you're already moving in the right direction for this career. The main things for aspiring writer's assistants to work on are their organizational skills and networking opportunities. Check out organizational tools that might be helpful to writers, whether it's online project management software like Trello or a writing program like Scrivener. Know how to book travel for someone and where to find the best deals. Being familiar with many different kinds of technology can be particularly useful. For instance, having at least a familiarity with microfiche can be helpful if you need to research something that hasn't been digitized yet. Knowing how to convert a VHS tape to a DVD or other digital format could help with making sure interviews get saved to the newest technology. But the basics are the

Writers' assistants take part in many important aspects of a writer's career, such as booking, publicity, and networking. Being familiar with different types of technology can make you more adept at that part of the job.

ADVICE FROM WRITER JUSTIN JORDAN

What attributes do you think are most helpful in a writer's assistant?

Being organized and reliable.

I am, and this is not, I think, unusual for writers, pretty good at being organized and reliable when it comes to writing. I am less so when it comes to pretty much everything else. So generally speaking, this is what I'm looking for in assistants, and I've used...uh....five, to date.

The reason I've used five is that I also use different assistants for specific tasks - I have an assistant who helps me man the table at cons, for instance, and another to help organize my financial records, and another for marketing, because these all require somewhat different skill sets (and, actually, geographic locations).

But the commonality is being organized and reliable.

What do you look for when hiring a writer's assistant?

Basically, aside from the above, I'm looking for ability to do the job and evidence we can actually get along. I think for these types of jobs, being able to get along is fairly important, and a general sense that we think about things kind of the same way. It's hard to delegate tasks to someone you don't like or don't understand.

What advice would you give to someone who wants to work as a writer's assistant?

Be pleasant, be professional, be organized and be reliable. And, on the flipsideflip side, don't work for jerks. Your job is to assist, but that doesn't mean you're a punching bag for abuse. Likewise, even when working with non-jerks, set the boundaries of the job very clearly. It's easy to drift, and it's easy to end up doing more than you're being paid to do, as well as ending up doing things you're not good at, which is bad for both parties.

same for all writers: know how to keep yourself organized and how to organize other people.

While some writers need full-time assistants, it's also worthwhile to speak with lesser-known writers who might need help for a few hours every week, or remote secretarial work once a month. It won't be enough to keep all of the bills paid, but many writer's assistants work with multiple writers, or do other freelance jobs like writing on their own or managing projects for other types of professionals. No matter what caliber of writer you work with, however, it's important that you maintain a professional attitude. Even if you're working with someone famous who has famous friends, you need to be able to keep your cool! Don't be too much of a fan.

For those who want to work as both a writer and an assistant, a decent knowledge of the writing craft is helpful. The writer you assist may want your input on their latest chapter, need you to write responses to their emails and letters, or even want to work with you on the projects you hope to publish. In these situations, you can learn on the job, but it's also good to be educating yourself on your own with writing manuals and style guides. Know what your writer prefers and learn how to interpret that into their writing, and your own, as needed.

CAREER POTENTIAL

Unfortunately there's no data on how many people work as writer's assistants in the United States, but with job growth expected for writers, it's safe to assume many of those writers will also need assistants. And as more people work with assistants online, it's entirely possible for this career to be conducted from anywhere. For those who love organization and research, this career could take you anywhere and lead to all sorts of interesting opportunities. You could remain a writer's assistant and become an expert at that, or you could use it as a stepping stone to a career of your own in writing, learning the ropes by assisting someone you admire. Also, a career as a writer's assistant can prepare you for other types of assistant and administrative jobs, as skills like organization, flexibility, and working with others are easily translatable across fields. Assisting writers could open all kinds of other doors career wise.

FOR MORE INFORMATION

ORGANIZATIONS

Association of Writers & Writing Programs
George Mason University
4400 University Drive
MSN 1E3
Fairfax, VA 22030
(703) 993-4301
Website: https://www.awpwriter.org
AWP provides support, advocacy, resources, and
community to nearly 50,000 writers, 550 college
and university creative writing programs, and 150
writers' conferences and centers.

International Writing Centers Association
705 Palomar Airport Road
Carlsbad, CA 92011
(760) 268-1567
Website: http://writingcenters.org
The International Writing Centers Association fosters
the development of writing center directors, tutors,
and staff by sponsoring meetings, publications,
and other professional activities; by encouraging

scholarship connected to writing center-related fields.

National Association of Independent Writers and Editors
P.O. Box 549
Ashland, Virginia 23005
(804) 767-5961
http://www.naiwe.com
A professional organization for writers in all genres, NAIWE connects writers and people who work with writers.

National Writers Association
10940 S. Parker Road, #508,
Parker, CO 80134
(303) 841-0246
http://www.nationawriters.com
Another professional organization for writers, the NWA could be an excellent place for a writer's assistant to make contacts.

The National Writers Union
256 West 38th Street, Suite 703
New York, NY 10018
(212) 254-0279
Website: http://www.nwu.org
An organization dedicated to protecting the rights
    of writers, NWU is a great resource for writer's
    assistants.

WEBSITES

Because of the changing nature of internet links, Rosen
Publishing has developed an online list of websites
related to the subject of this book. This site is updated
regularly. Please use this link to access the list:

http://www.rosenlinks.com/CCWC/reading

CHAPTER 5

SHARING WHAT YOU LOVE: A CAREER AS A BOOKSTORE OWNER

If you love to read, bookstores are often one of the very best places in the world. The amazing news is that you can work in one and feed your reading habit all day long. There is a wide range of jobs available at bookstores, from being a clerk or sales associate to owning your own shop. In between there are options to be a book buyer for a bookstore or a bookstore manager. And the size and kind of bookstore varies, too, from large general stores like Barnes & Noble to niche stores like a comic book store or a small travel book store. Plus, there are bookstores all over the world, so

A book lover can find many job opportunities in bookstores. From clerk to manager to book buyer to owner, there are many different ways to participate in the business of bookselling.

there are opportunities in this career everywhere from in your hometown or across the globe.

It's important to remember that it's not as simple as loving books, however—working in a bookstore also requires a lot of customer service and a strong knowledge of the book market. The former will require a lot of patience, while the latter will require a lot of research into current and future trends.

PREPARING YOURSELF

If you plan to work your way up from the bottom in this career, much of what you need to know will be learned on the job. You can start right now, even before you graduate high school, and work part-time in a bookstore to start building your knowledge. The best way to know what goes on in a bookstore on the day-to-day is to be a sales associate. You'll see how the customers react to the business, how to make them happy or angry, and how sales move at different times of the day, week, and year. You'll even be able to watch trends as they happen on the sales floor. This knowledge will be helpful if you want to manage the bookstore you're working in or if you plan to open a similar bookstore in another area. It may not seem glamorous, but it can lead to a long career, if you want it to.

A book buyer should have a solid familiarity with the trends that are happening in publishing, especially as many publishers ask for orders far ahead of when the books will actually be on shelves. This is a very important position in retail and can be challenging, but someone who has a good knowledge of the book market should be able to do a good job. For a buyer, the most important thing is their knowledge of the entire book market and how that applies to their store in particular. This will require a head for research and reading, as well as some sort of understanding of the retail business.

But if you want to jump up to the level of owner or manager, you're going to need to have a head for business. It's no easy task managing a store, and you'll want to know some of the basics of accounting, how to create business plans, how the bookstore was managed before, and more. Being a small business owner is particularly challenging, as it can take a long time for a business to make a profit. Bookstores, in particular, are not a business known for making their owners wealthy. The good news is that there are a lot of resources out there for those who want to learn, from free seminars with local business associations to websites to books. This is another area where having a mentor can be helpful, if you work with someone who you admire and whose career you'd like to emulate. It's not just about understanding bookstores, either. You should be prepared to understand larger retail trends and objectives in order to stay competitive.

The American Booksellers Association (ABA) is a great place to start in your research. It offers a great deal of information about the state of bookselling today as well as information relevant to aspiring booksellers. If you join the ABA, you get many benefits that can help you start or run your bookstore. You can request an information packet right now if you want to. It's an excellent resource for anyone who wants to own a bookstore or even just manage one.

Another great resource is Paz & Associates' Bookstore Training Group, which offers workshops and other resources, including online classes. There's even an

There are lots of different types of bookstores, from small independent shops with a family feel to large national chains that offer opportunities for corporate employment.

"Owning A Bookstore" workshop retreat where you can go to learn all about every aspect of running a bookstore. It's great to have some background in working in a bookstore before you splurge on a workshop like this, but if you're wanting to advance your career to the next step, it's a wonderful resource. It's also a lot cheaper than college.

CAREER POTENTIAL

There's no limit here—you could end up working in the corporate offices of Barnes & Noble or running your very own bookstore. While bookstores have faltered in the last decade, retail jobs are showing growth over the next decade. Plus, sales trends currently show that book sales have increased over the last few years, so it's a good time to work in the book business. While many assumed that e-books would challenge brick-and-mortar bookstores, people still shop at bookstores and use them as meeting places for their community. Especially if you want to specialize in a niche, now is a good time to work in a bookstore and help spread your love of reading to others. Additionally, the rise of popularity in digital publishing and online sales does not have to be a negative thing for an aspiring bookseller. You could capitalize on the popularity of e-books by starting your own site that sells digital literature, or you could run your own online business selling physical books. Many people supplement or earn their incomes by selling books on Amazon, Ex Libris, Barnes & Noble, and other websites with a sales platform. This could be your endgame, or it could be a way to get started in the book business and earn the revenue that would allow you to open a physical store. The possibilities in book sales are endless, varied and flexible, making it an excellent reading and research career to pursue without a college degree.

FOR MORE INFORMATION

ORGANIZATIONS

American Booksellers Association
333 Westchester Avenue
Suite S202
White Plains, NY 10604
(800) 637-0037
Website: http://www.bookweb.org
The ABA is a nonprofit trade organization that promotes
the success of independent booksellers.

The Antiquarian Booksellers Association of America
20 West 44th Street, #507
New York, NY 10036
(212) 944-8291
Website: http://www.abaa.org
The ABAA is a trade association for sellers of used and
rare books.

Retail Council of Canada
Toronto Office
1881 Yonge Street
Suite 800
Toronto, ON M4S 3C4
Canada
Website: http://www.retailcouncil.org

The Retail Council of Canada represents the Canadian Booksellers Association, the country's largest professional organization for booksellers.

BOOKS

Drenth, Tere Stouffer. *Bookselling For Dummies.* Hoboken, NJ: Wiley, 2005.
Laties, Andrew. *Rebel Bookseller: Why Independent Bookstores Represent Everything You Want to Fight for from Free Speech to Buying Local to Building Communities.* New York, NY: Seven Stories Press, 2011.
Vines, Andy. *The Bookshop Diaries: Confessions of a Bookseller.* Amazon Digital Services: Kindle Edition, 2016.

WEBSITES

Because of the changing nature of internet links, Rosen Publishing has developed an online list of websites related to the subject of this book. This site is updated regularly. Please use this link to access the list:

http://www.rosenlinks.com/CCWC/reading

CHAPTER 6

SHHH!! A CAREER AS A LIBRARY TECH

Many people know that to be a librarian you have to have a masters in library science, but what most don't know is that it's possible to work in a library and not be a librarian! Most public and school libraries now use library aides or librarian assistants who do a lot of things that a librarian does, but are more affordable for the libraries. City libraries may have as many as dozens of librarian assistants who work the checkout counter, the information desk, and restock books. Some school districts have only one librarian who visits each school on a

Just like a career in a bookstore, a job in a library allows you to spend your work days physically surrounded by books. Library work also provides an excellent opportunity to exercise your love of research.

different day, while the bulk of the day-to-day work is being done by a library tech.

Having a love of reading and research is obviously helpful for those who want to work in a library. If you love books, it makes sense to spend your days surrounded by them, but you should also want to help others with their research and reading needs. Customer service is a big part of working in a library and is a key component of the work of a library assistant or library aide. For those working in school libraries, you should be prepared to work with children of various ages and reading levels, which can be challenging but also rewarding.

INTERVIEW WITH CHRISTINA "STEENZ" STEWART, LIBRARY TECHNICIAN

What are the most important qualities you look for when working with a librarian assistant/library aide?
When looking for an aide, the most important quality is the ability to follow through with tasks. Then comes legible handwriting. When writing where you left off on a project, the next person that takes over has to know what to do next.

What advice would you give someone who wanted to work in a
library but couldn't afford to or didn't want to go to college?
Keep applying. Find out what the library needs and try to fill
that role more so than just applying to do a particular job.
I don't have my degree in library sciences or anything, but I
offered community contacts and a history of event planning.
So my title is "library tech," but I do the work of a programming librarian.

Do you have an undergraduate degree?
Nope. I have three years of an art degree, but five years of
programming experience. But I'm never going to be able to
get paid more than I do or get a promotion because of it. So
if you have the money to get a degree, do it. But if not, you
kinda have to surrender to the notion that you won't get
paid well.

What are your favorite parts of what you do?
This question will be different depending on what librarian
you talk to, but I know I enjoy spreading knowledge and
entertainment to those who cannot afford it. I like how quiet
it is in the reference section. I like working on projects that
are creative and push the idea the libraries have evolved to
be a community center more than just a place of reference.

PREPARING YOURSELF

If you're interested in being a librarian assistant, it's a good idea to familiarize yourself with how libraries work. Spend some time in your local libraries and see how they're organized. Understand and learn the difference between things like the Dewey Decimal System and the Library of Congress system, as each can impact how the books in a library are arranged. Being good at alphabetizing is obviously a very useful skill, as well. Sometimes, schools

The Library of Congress, housed in this building, created one of the systems by which books are organized in libraries. It is important to be familiar with this system and with the Dewey Decimal System if you want to work in a library.

will let students help out in the library during a study hall, and this is a good way to learn how the library works.

To be fair, if you're an avid reader, you're probably already familiar with how a library works. When you're ready to look for work at your local library, start at the city government pages. Many library jobs are listed there. But you may have to wait to find exactly the right position for your skill set.

The American Library Association (ALA) also suggests that librarian assistants also be familiar with computers—which makes a lot of sense! After all, a great deal of the work done in libraries these days involves computers. It's a good idea to not only understand computers and how to work on them, but to also be prepared to explain some computer basics to unfamiliar users. One of the tasks many librarian assistants deal with is helping customers with the computer systems, either to find a book or to access the internet or online archives of some sort. If you have your eye on working in a particular city's library, it's not a bad idea to spend some time with their computers and understand how they work.

If your dream is to work in a library, but you can't find a job right away, it might also help to work in other clerical jobs while you look for a library job. Any position that requires computer skills, customer service, alphabetizing, filing, etc. can look great on a resume while applying to be a librarian assistant. As Stewart mentions in the sidebar, knowing how to organize community events is also an important skill that can be an asset for a library tech. Libraries are often used as venues for meetings, readings, and other public gatherings, so event planning can put you in high demand for working at a library.

CAREER POTENTIAL

Thankfully, libraries are a lasting part of our society and they continue to grow—but not every library can afford a full staff of librarians. The growth rates for library workers who are not librarians far outpaces the growth rates for librarian jobs, which means it's easier to get

From helping others to find books to shelving quietly in the stacks, working in a library is an excellent way to earn a living through your love of reading and books.

hired as a non-college educated library worker than it is to get hired as a full librarian. This is great news for those of you reading the information contained in these sections. It means you have an excellent chance of finding a great job at a library without worrying about going to college. You can be surrounded by books on a daily basis, and earn your living by working in an ideal location for indulging your interest in reading and research.

FOR MORE INFORMATION

ORGANIZATIONS

American Library Association
50 East Huron Street
Chicago, Illinois 60611-2795
Website: http://www.ala.org
The oldest and largest library association in
   the world, ALA fosters the development,
   improvement and promotion of library and
   information services.

Atlantic Provinces Library Association
Dalhousie University
Kenneth C. Rowe Management Building
6100 University Avenue
Suite 4010 PO Box 15000
Halifax, NS B3H 4R2
Canada
Website: http://www.apla.ca/
APLA is a Canadian association that serves the interests
   of library workers in the region.

Library of Congress
101 Independence Avenue, SE
Washington, DC 20540
(202) 707-5000
Website: https://www.loc.gov/
The Library of Congress is the largest library in
the world, with millions of books, recordings,
photographs, newspapers, maps and manuscripts in
its collections.

Ontario Association of Library Technicians
Abbey Market, P.O. Box 76010,
1500 Upper Middle Road West,
Oakville, ON, L6M 3H5
Canada
Website: https://oaltabo.on.ca/
OALT is a non-profit organization of graduates in the
field of library and information services.

BOOKS

Cassell, Kay Anne. *Reference and Information Services:
An Introduction*. Third Edition. Chicago, IL: ALA,
2012.

Johnson, Anne. *Library Technician Career: The Insider's Guide to Finding a Job at an Amazing Firm, Acing The Interview & Getting Promoted.* CreateSpace, 2016.
Keeler, Hali R. *Foundations of Library Services: An Introduction for Support Staff.* Lanham, MD: Rowman and Littlefield, 2015.

WEBSITES

Because of the changing nature of internet links, Rosen Publishing has developed an online list of websites related to the subject of this book. This site is updated regularly. Please use this link to access the list:

http://www.rosenlinks.com/CCWC/reading

CHAPTER 7

BACK TO YOUR ROOTS: A CAREER AS A GENEALOGIST

One of the most fascinating and unique careers for those who love reading and research is to work as a genealogist. Particularly if you are interested in history, genealogy can be a rich career full of interesting discoveries. In recent years, thanks to the rise of websites like Ancestry.com, a lot of people are taking an interest in their family roots. But not everyone is a skilled researcher,

A genealogist can help people discover long lost information about and photographs of their ancestors, and help their clients to put together their family stories.

and so many people like to hire professional genealogists to assist in their research.

There are a lot of ways that genealogists are hired, but most of them work on a freelance, job-by-job basis. The Association of Professional Genealogists offers the ability to hire a professional genealogist through their website, and local genealogy societies offer similar connections. The Association of Professional Genealogists is also the primary association for those who want to be able to

JEAN WILCOX HIBBEN; PHD, MA, CG®

What sort of skills do you think are important for a genealogist to have?

Patience, resourcefulness, willingness to contact strangers and tough skin when they refuse an interview or to give you assistance, communication techniques for interviews and to get access to records. Of course, good, solid research skills are a must. Good English (or whatever) language with excellent spelling, punctuation, and syntax for report writing is important, along with willingness to take direction from those who are more experienced (that's good for any occupation).

What advice would you give someone who is was considering becoming a professional genealogist?

Attend as many workshops, classes, seminars, and conferences as possible. Also join the Association of Professional Genealogists IMMEDIATELY upon deciding on this as a possible career. You need not be a professional to join the organization and there is a student membership rate. From that group you get help from their publications, webinars, mailing list, and more. Plus you get familiar with the "names" in the field and can contact those people directly for suggestions (just don't be a pest). Choosing 2 or 3 people as mentors (whether they know it or not), buying and reading their publications, subscribing to their blogs, attending their webinars, etc. will all help the student grow in his/her desired area of the field. Find a niche that works for you (mine is folklore, social history, and their connections to ancestry) and then choose mentors who specialize in those areas (e.g., DNA research, PI work, photo specialty, particular military history, etc.). You might also onsider taking classes to help strengthen your research skills. Some are more expensive than others, but all will help with growth in the field. I also strongly recommend never to take a client or a booking that you know is out of your area of expertise. Unless you are just helping a friend and/or to learn, it's more likely to create problems if you have to take lots of additional time to do research and, if it's for a client, charging for your learning curve is hardly ethical. Suggest a better person for the job or recommend the APG website for the potential client to check.

Let me add, a genealogist must be his/her own advocate. It's hard to step up and say, "I am the person you want to hire," but, if that's the case, you need to do it. Set up a website and/or blog to get your name out there and make it exclusive to your business. Your email address should reflect that you are a serious genealogist, not a hobbyist. Lovemygrandkids@abc.com is not as effective as Grandparent_hunter@abc.com. It may sound like a simple thing, but it makes a difference to someone looking to hire a professional. Make your business cards on a light-colored card stock with place on front or back for people to make notes. Cards printed on dark colored stock look cool, but are rarely effective in many other ways. And have folks proofread your material.

And just be sure to make sure that your business cards reflect accurately what you do and your location. A friend does his research in New England, commonly abbreviated NE. But I'm from the Midwest and immediately assumed he specialized in Nebraska research. I have no idea if he has lost clients because of it, but it's entirely possible.

What is your favorite part of being a genealogist?

Personally, I love taking research I've done and creating instructional presentations for people who might not be aware of some of my resources. I love talking to people about their family stories and trying to help them verify them. And I like networking with other genealogists for new ideas and just sharing those "let me tell you about this weird case" experiences.

call themselves professional genealogists. Ancestry.com, however, offers something called ProGenealogists, which is based in Salt Lake City, Utah, and where genealogists work on staff. If you want something a little more stable than the traditional freelance model, this is a potentially good option.

PREPARING YOURSELF

A great way to prepare yourself for a career in genealogy is to start researching your own family. Learn the ropes using a story you're personally invested in and it can help you understand what the people you'd be helping would be looking for. It's not as simple as digging up facts and information—being a genealogist is also about assisting people in finding a connection to their ancestors. Being a dedicated researcher can really help in this arena, especially if you have an interest in working with older documents that haven't yet been digitized. Genealogy may require you to spend time perusing dusty old journals and papers or combing through microfilm at the library.

Understanding history is also extremely important to genealogists—after all, your clients may not. Many times the job requires explaining events to those without a strong grasp of history and it will be your job to explain

Genealogy can lead to all kinds of interesting research. Here, a genealogist poses with an architect. The two are doing joint research to document cemeteries in Arkansas.

what their ancestors were doing and why. History is a key part of genealogy and so many genealogists read extensively about history. This is one reason why some genealogists have specialties; it's impossible to know everything that ever happened in history, so a genealogist might choose to study only local history, or one part of local history as it relates to a larger emigration, or some specific era and location. Genealogists often start off in an area that is of their own particular interest, and build their specialty from there. Having a strong knowledge of a particular period or periods in history can help you to bring your clients into a personal connection with their ancestors. This makes discoveries much more meaningful and personal.

From dusty old books to archived photos to microfilm, genealogy will allow you to research all kinds of old documents, opening the door to lost stories and new understanding.

Going to your local gene-alogical society and learning about their resources can also be very helpful. Many large cities have these kinds of soci-eties, and a lot of them have a particular area of research based on the local population. If you live in an area where your family has lived for a few generations, this can be a great resource. Plus, it's a great way to meet working genealogists, and if you enjoy the work and want to do it professionally, you can join the society and become a professional geneal-ogist. Some genealogists spend their days at the genealogical society, waiting for requests for research assistance to come through.

Watching shows like Who Do You Think You Are? can also help you understand the kind of narrative that you get to tell when relating events to clients. It also allows you to see professional genealogists in action, interacting with their customers. Granted, it's a television episode, so it's not necessarily going to show the entire process, but it's still a decent look at the end results of what genealogists do. Telling a story is a key part of being a genealogist, as you connect the dots between bits of information and assist the customer in seeing the story of their ancestor's life. You help your client to connect the dots that lead from the ancestors in question to your client's own life in modern times. Watching the narratives created by genealogical television shows can help you to learn how to create meaningful narratives for your clients, making the experience more poignant for them and for you.

CAREER POTENTIAL

Unfortunately, there's not a lot of data regarding the genealogist job market, but it's safe to say the growth of the internet has made it an increasingly popular career for those interested in history and research. Ancestry.com has a booming business and is using it to increase awareness of genealogical research, which in turn seems to make being a genealogist a more popular career than it ever has been before. It's also a career that can be done while also doing other things, like any of the other options in this book. Genealogy can be your full-time focus, or it can be a something you do on the side to supplement your main income. Who knows, you might even end up hosting your own genealogy blog, video web series, or television show. No matter how you choose to do it, working in genealogy involves lots of research and reading about historical and scientific topics, and is an excellent choice for someone who loves to do these things but does not want to get caught up in the debt and the time commitment involved in trying to obtain a full-fledged college degree. It is worth very serious consideration.

FOR MORE INFORMATION

ORGANIZATIONS

American-Canadian Genealogical Society
4 Elm Street
Manchester, NH 03103
(603) 622-1554
Website: http://www.acgs.org
Founded in 1973, NCGS seeks to unite members of the
genealogical community from around the world.

Association of Professional Genealogists
PO Box 535
Wheat Ridge, CO 80034-0535
(303) 465-6980
Website: http://www.apgen.org
This organization supports the work of amateur
genealogists as well as drawing together those that
work in the field professionally.

National Genealogical Society
3108 Columbia Pike, Suite 300
Arlington, Virginia 22204-4370 USA
(800) 473-0060
Website: http://www.nsgenealogy.org

NGS provides education and training to support the genealogical community.

BOOKS

Bettinger, Blaine T. *The Family Tree Guide to DNA Testing and Genetic Genealogy.* Family Tree Books, 2016.
Hendrickson, Nancy. *Unofficial Guide to Ancestry.com.* Family Tree Books, 2014.
Smith, Drew. *Organize Your Genealogy: Strategies and Solutions For Every Researcher.* Family Tree Books, 2016.

WEBSITES

Because of the changing nature of internet links, Rosen Publishing has developed an online list of websites related to the subject of this book. This site is updated regularly. Please use this link to access the list:

http://www.rosenlinks.com/CCWC/reading

CHAPTER 8

BRIEFED: A CAREER AS A LEGAL SECRETARY

Many people think of legal careers as requireing a great deal of education, but there's one important part of the legal proffession that can be done with only a high school diploma—that of the legal secretary. Legal secretaries do a great deal of research and reading to assist lawyers with the work they do. There's also, of course, a lot of administrative work, as with other secretarial jobs, but legal secretaries can be very important to the overall legal process. While a lawyer may not have the time to read through endless legal codes, they might ask their secretary to look for a

You don't have to spend years in college and go thousands of dollars into debt to have a career in the legal field. Legal secretaries do not have to have any particular certification.

particular bit of information. This is a great career option for anyone who loves reading and research, and the law. Unlike a paralegal, a legal secretary does not have to have any specialized certification. He or she simply needs to have the experience or the potential to be an effective administrative assistant and to handle the research and writing tasks that the boss may require.

DRAFTING LEGAL DOCUMENTS

There are very specific rules involved in writing legal documents, and anyone who aspires to be a legal secretary should be familiar with them. Many of these rules apply to all writing, but in legal documents it is imperative that they are followed. Any writer should strive to be clear and direct, but when composing legal documents, clumsy wording could result in the rejection of a proposal or the loss of a case. There are several elements that the writer of a legal document must consider. These elements include but are not limited to:

Arrangement: The document must be divided into sections that each have a clear topic, and items must be logically arranged within each topic.

Ambiguity: In all types of writing, but especially legal writing, ambiguity can create serious problems with meaning.

Definitions: In many types of legal documents, an appendix with definitions of terms may be necessary.

Format requirements: Be familiar with the specific format requirements for the type of document you are writing. A grant proposal, for instance, has a very different structure from a legal brief.

Punctuation, capitalization, typography and spelling: Mechanics are important in every type of writing, but in legal documents a comma or a period in the wrong place could render the document useless.

Principles of clear writing: Write in the active voice rather than the passive voice, use must rather than shall, use the present tense whenever possible, write positively, avoid the use of exceptions, use the singular rather than the plural, be consistent with the terms you choose, use parallel construction, avoid redundancies and gender-specific language, use short paragraphs, and make the structure of your lists logical and clear.

If you aspire to become a legal secretary, it would be wise to practice and become familiar with , elements of a good legal document.

PREPARING YOURSELF

It's important to have some knowledge of the law if you would like to work as a legal secretary. Reading books about legal cases that interest you and making connections in the legal community can help. It may be difficult to get work as a legal secretary straight out of high school, however, since these jobs come with considerable responsibility. In this case, it can be good to work as a regular secretary or receptionist for a few years to get some experience in the administrative tasks you might be required to understand.

Having a knowledge of basic computer programs like Microsoft Word and Excel is important to any secretarial position, and that's true for legal secretaries as well. Being good at tasks like filing and alphabetizing will help as well. And being organized is a great skill for any kind of secretary, as well.

But the most important part of being a legal secretary is what makes it different from other kinds of secretarial or administrative positions: the research. A legal secretary should be capable of detailed research as, depending on the client and case, it could literally be a matter of life or death. Much of a legal secretary's research will involve reading and interpreting laws, and this can be a daunting task. One thing that would be helpful in preparing yourself is to develop a working knowledge of the Latin terms that appear in legal books, such as a priori (from earlier), ad hominem (at the person), and bona fide (in good faith). Another good idea is to research important Supreme Court cases in order to be familiar with the precedents they set. Additionally, it would be wise to assemble a list of reliable online sources for legal research. The internet is rife with unreliable sources, and a good legal secretary knows the legitimate ones from the ones that should be disregarded. All of these preparations can be cited on a resume, and you can refer to them in interviews as evidence that you make an ideal legal secretary.

CAREER POTENTIAL

Gaining experience as a legal secretary can open lots of doors for future career potential. Because being a legal secretary requires specialized knowledge that other secretarial work does not, any law firm will be more likely to hire a secretary with previous experience in the field. Because legal documents are not structured the same way as other kinds of documents, law firms are much more enthusiastic to hire someone who has written them before and is familiar with their unique structure. Therefore, once you gain a year or two of experience, you will open up plenty of opportunities for yourself to potentially be hired at other firms. Additionally, if you decide that you want to add to your professionalism by becoming certified as a paralegal, you can do so with only a couple of years of further education; most paralegals have only an associate's degree. A legal secretary is a fantastic career choice for someone who wants a high-demand position that does not require college, but that does, at the same time, pave the way for the possibility of further education in the future. Additionally, many of the skills involved in being a legal secretary, such as the ability to communicate clearly

You might remain a legal secretary or become a certified paralegal (which also does not take much schooling). There are lots of opportunities in the legal field.

(especially in writing), the ability to work under pressure, the ability to develop and understand logical arguments, and the ability to conduct effective research, easily translate to other fields outside of the legal profession. This career provides flexibility within the field and opens doors outside of it.

FOR MORE INFORMATION

ORGANIZATIONS

Legal Secretaries International Inc.
2951 Marina Bay Dr., Ste. 130-641
League City, TX 77573
Website: http://www.legalsecretaries.org
This organization strives to improve the professional
   lives of legal secretaries through education and
   networking.

Ontario Paralegal Association
400 Applewood Crescent, Suite #100
Vaughan Ontario L4K 0C3
(416) 944-1020
Website: http://www.ontarioparralegalassociation.com
While this association is for licensed paralegals, it could
   also be a valuable resource for legal secretaries in the
   Ontario area.

San Francisco Legal Professionals Association
P.O. Box 2582
San Francisco, CA 94126-2582
(415) 585-7792
Website: http://www.sflpa.org

This organization offers guidance and leadership to the legal professional community in the San Francisco area.

BOOKS

Foley, Ashley. *Steps To Becoming a Paralegal*. Amazon Digital Publishing Services, 2014.

Hatch, Sue. *Paralegal Career For Dummies*. Amazon Digital Services, 2011.

Paschall, Cordy. *The Legal Secretary Guide*. Hudson, OH: PAS Publishing, 2012.

WEBSITES

Because of the changing nature of internet links, Rosen Publishing has developed an online list of websites related to the subject of this book. This site is updated regularly. Please use this link to access the list:

http://www.rosenlinks.com/CCWC/reading

CHAPTER 9

SOMETHING OLD: A CAREER AS AN ANTIQUES DEALER

Much like genealogists, those who buy and sell antiques are often history buffs who love to read and research the individual stories behind history. But unlike genealogists, antique dealers focus on objects rather than people. This is a good career for those interested in furniture, jewelry, glassware, and really any kind of object that has some sort of history. There are antique stores everywhere, too, so while the well-known antiques auction houses may seem limited to major cities, smaller cities may still have a thriving antiques market. And even small towns can support a simple antique business.

Two people pose at a flea market in Paris. Flea markets are one of the main places where antiques dealers can buy and sell their wares.

One of the best parts about working with antiques is that you can choose what is most interesting to you. Do you love late 19th century tables? There's a market for that. Do you obsess over 1950s Bakelite jewelry? There's a market for that, too. Learning what particular kind of objects you're interested in is a great place to start in the world of antiques. To learn what you're interested in, well, reading is a good place to start—read about furniture makers of the early 20th century or the popular plate styles of 1930s Chicago. The options are endless. Whatever you want to specialize in, though, reading about and understanding the historical context of the items you want to buy and sell is very important.

PREPARING YOURSELF

Once you know what you're interested in, visiting antique stores to get a sense for how things are priced in your area, as well asand reading pricing guides and researching prices online. Visiting antiques stores can also be helpful for finding work in this arena. You could get a position as a store clerk or a store manager as your way to breaking into buying and selling antiques on your own. Even if you don't get work at the local antiques store, many offer stalls for rent, so if you develop an inventory of your own, you could always rent a stall at the antiques store.

Another good place to start is to attend local auctions and estate sales. You'll be able to see what people are willing to spend in that context, and compare it with the retail prices you've researched. If you want to invest in some pieces, this is a good place to start. If you want to get into antiques restoration, this is a particularly good place to look as you can find broken pieces that are still salvageable to those in the know. You probably won't have a lot of competition for the broken pieces unless you're in a market with a lot of knowledgeable antique restorers. This is also a good place to see what sells in your area. People in certain geographic areas may like vintage farm equipment as home decor, for instance, but in other areas mid-century modern curios might be the hottest pieces. If you do want to run your own antique store, this is where you can get a good idea of what you'll want to sell in your store.

Finally, like becoming a bookstore owner, being an antiques dealer that is also a small business owner can be extremely challenging. It's important to have some understanding of good business practices and how to run a business, which can be learned by reading business books and journals. It's possible to be a casual antique seller, but you'll also want to make sure you set aside enough for taxes, for instance. Research on this topic is

Antique dealers find lost and forgotten treasures and connect their customers with these finds. They often do all kinds of interesting research to discover the stories behind these treasures.

really important. If you are not properly prepared and informed, your antique dealing could wind up costing you money instead of increasing your revenue. However, with adequate preparation and information, it can be a very lucrative pursuit.

CAREER POTENTIAL

Antiques are not of interest to everyone, but they are a constant in our society. As time goes on, more and more things become antiques, so eventually even the objects of your youth will become collectible for someone. It can be a challenging career, but it's one that can be rewarding and can lead to owning your own antiques business. You might run a business online in which you store the antiques in your home and simply market them through pictures and descriptions on existing websites. You might design your own website through which to market your wares. Or you might open up a brick-and-mortar store, applying your creativity and business savvy to create an inviting and profitable physical space to sell your antiques. No matter which option you choose, antique dealing will allow you to indulge in your passion for reading and research without having to earn any particular degree or certification.

FOR MORE INFORMATION

ORGANIZATIONS

Antiques & Collectibles National Association
PO Box 4389
Davidson, NC 28036
Website: http://www.antiqueandcollectible.com
The Antiques & Collectibles National Association
has become the largest industry association with
thousands of members in all 50 states to provide
benefits to antique dealers and private collectors.

Antiques Dealers' Association of America
P. O. Box 218
Northwood, NH 03261
(603) 942-6498
Website: http://www.adadealers.com
This organization has over 100 members who are all
antiques dealers.

Appraisers Association of America, Inc.
212 West 35th Street
11th Floor South
New York, NY 10001
(212) 889-5503

Website: http://www.appraisersassociation.org

The Appraisers Association of America, established in 1949, is the premier national association of personal property appraisers who focus on fine and decorative arts.

Canadian Antique Dealers Association
211, Cherry Hill Rd
PO Box 81
Grafton, Ontario K0K 2G0
Canada
(416) 972-1378
Website: http://www.cadainfo.com/

This organization ensures the quality of antique dealing in Canada by providing its seal to approved businesses.

National Art and Antiques Dealers Association of America
220 East 57th Street
New York, NY 10022
Website: http://www.naadaa.org/

NAADA is a non-profit trade association of experienced and vetted dealers who provide advice and support to one another.

BOOKS

Bingham, Joan. *Buying and Selling Antiques and Collectibles For Fun and Profit.* Vermont: Tuttle Publishing, 2012.

Czerkawska, Catherine. *Precious Vintage: Making Money From Antiques and Collectibles.* Wordarts, 2014.

White, Edward. *How To Profit From Buying and Selling Antiques.* Amazon Digital Services, 2012.

WEBSITES

Because of the changing nature of internet links, Rosen Publishing has developed an online list of websites related to the subject of this book. This site is updated regularly. Please use this link to access the list:

http://www.rosenlinks.com/CCWC/reading

CHAPTER 10

DIGITAL NATIVE: A CAREER AS A BLOGGER

Although it can be a tough field to break into, there are millions of people making money as bloggers—and blogging requires absolutely no specific educational preparation or certification. Additionally, blogging can begin as a hobby and can eventually lead to making money, so it is a perfect long-term goal to focus on while you do something else. There are countless different blogs on the internet, with countless varied focuses. For a person who loves reading and research, blogging could be an ideal way to exercise that love and turn it into a profitable enterprise. You could review books,

Because blogging can be done at any time and from any place, and because posts can be as short or as long as you want them to be, it is one of the most flexible writing careers there is.

blog about the latest research in a particular field, blog about visits to various libraries and archives, conduct field research and chronicle your travels…the possibilities are

HOW BLOGGING BEGAN

The website that is officially considered the very first blog was started by a man named Justin Hall in 1994, while Hall attended Swarthmore College in Swarthmore, PennsylvaniaA. Hall's site still exists online now at www.links.net, and although he has incorporated some modern elements into the blog, it still maintains a simple layout reminiscent of the original. Another early blogger named John Barger simply kept a record of websites that he visited during his web browsing. Barger coined the term "web log" in 1997. Eventually, the term was shortened to "blog," and it stuck. In addition to the early sites keeping track of web browsing, many early internet users maintained online diaries of their daily events and musings, or wrote about music and other entertainment forms. When blogging tools like Livejournal and Blogger came onto the scene, blogging became increasingly popular because it was more accessible to people with a talent for writing but with limited technical skills. Since then, the popularity of blogs has increased to the point that many news and entertainment sites contain blogs as a regular feature, and many independent bloggers have been awarded book deals. Blogging has emerged from its humble roots to become a viable career choice rather than just a simple hobby.

endless. Blogging requires minimal preparation and the money-making potential is great! Even better, you can start to build your blog immediately!

PREPARING YOURSELF

In preparation for earning a living by blogging, just as in any other career, you should study and learn from the people who have already found success in the profession. Choose a few blogs that you enjoy and that have taken off, and analyze what those bloggers are doing. If possible, find a mentor who you can turn to for advice and whose practices you can mirror.

If you are truly committed to making your living as a blogger, you might initially want to maintain more than one blog. Although it will take a lot of work, this increases the possibility that one of them will take off. Create blogs that fit a couple of different niches, and see which one begins to pick up the most traffic. Eventually, when it becomes clear that one is generating more interest than the other, you can abandon the one that isn't performing as well. Alternatively, you could continue to maintain them both, in the hope that the slower one will pick up speed in the future.

Whatever niche you choose, you will need to stay up to date with developments in the relevant area. For instance, if you blog about fashion, you will need to determine some sources that will help keep you up to date in the fashion industry. If you blog about music, you will need to follow some music columnists who you turn to for reviews and recommendations. If you blog about fitness, you will need to keep abreast of new developments in exercise and nutrition. Becoming an expert and an informed participant in the field you intend to blog about is an excellent way to prepare yourself for blogging as a possible career.

CAREER POTENTIAL

While you will not be able to make a living solely from blogging overnight, some people are definitely able to

Bloggers research and write about all kinds of different topics. The more you read and researrch, the more you have to comment on and write about!

earn a full-time income from this pursuit. In addition to earning revenue from a blog itself, many bloggers are able to parlay their blogs into book deals, online video series, or even television shows. The key to realizing the career potential in blogging is patience and perseverance. In the article "How to Make a Living At Blogging" on Forbes.com, Dorie Clark reports on successful blogger Matt Kepnes' advice to aspiring bloggers. Kepnes says that you should assume you won't make any money in the beginning. Clark says that it took Kepnes eighteen months to be able to live primarily off of his blog, and six years before he made enough to hire employees. However, by following several strategies, including finding a clear niche, making multiple revenue streams, and building a professional community, Kepnes was able to turn blogging into a full-fledged career. If you are able to do the same, you can open all kinds of doors for yourself and create a professional life where you set your own hours and work from anywhere you want, traveling, writing, and making connections. Your blog can be an expression of who you are as well as a source of income. It can be the perfect way to meld your personal and professional lives.

If you enjoy writing as well as research, there are many possible career paths you can take that do not require a college degree. While college can be a great experience and a wise choice for people who hope to follow certain career paths, it can be an incredibly costly pursuit and can drive you into debt before you even begin your life as an adult professional. If you can see yourself following one of the career paths described here, you may be able to get a head start and avoid wasting time and incurring unnecessary loans. If this seems like a good plan for you, begin preparing yourself today.

FOR MORE INFORMATION

ORGANIZATIONS

Association of Writers & Writing Programs
George Mason University
4400 University Drive
MSN 1E3
Fairfax, VA 22030
(703) 993-4301
Website: https://www.awpwriter.org
AWP provides support, advocacy, resources, and
    community to nearly 50,000 writers, 550 college and
    university creative writing programs, and 150 writers'
    conferences and centers.

International Bloggers' Association
PO BOX 193
Elizabethtown, KY 42702
Website: http://www.internationalbloggersassociation.
    com/
Founded in 2014 by blogger Brittany Bullen, IBA
    connects and supports bloggers from all walks of life.

BOOKS

Hirsch, Efron. *Blogging: The Ultimate Guide On How to Replace Your Job With a Blog.* CreateSpace Independent Publishing, 2016.

Lim, David. *Blogging: How To Start a Profitable Blog.* Amazon Digital Services, 2014.

Pipps, Karen G. *The Absolute Blogging How-To Handbook For New Bloggers.* CreateSpace Independent Publishing, 2011.

WEBSITES

Because of the changing nature of internet links, Rosen Publishing has developed an online list of websites related to the subject of this book. This site is updated regularly. Please use this link to access the list:

http://www.rosenlinks.com/CCWC/reading

GLOSSARY

AGENT a person who acts on behalf of another; in writing and other art forms, a person who promotes your work on your behalf.

ASPIRING wanting to do or become.

BRICK-AND-MORTAR a physical store as opposed to a catalog or online store.

COMMISSION to give an order for or authorize production of something (a book, for instance).

DEWEY DECIMAL SYSTEM a cataloging system for books in a library.

ETHICS moral principles that govern ones actions and decisions, or the study of those principles.

FREELANCE self-employed, working on a contract or job-by-job basis.

LIVETWEET to document something on Twitter in real time as it is happening.

GENEALOGY the study and tracing of lines of decent.

GENRE a category of art forms such as music and writing.

GIST the basic idea of something.

LEGIBLE able to be read.

MENTOR a teacher and role model.

MISCONCEPTION an incorrect belief.

NETWORKING socializing with people in your field or a related field in order to make professional connections.

NICHE a particular place or position.

PERUSE to look over.

PROSE writing that is not poetry or lyrics.

PERSEVERANCE fortitude; not giving up.

RUDIMENTARY basic.

BIBLIOGRAPHY

American Booksellers. www.bookweb.org. Retrieved November 18, 2016. www.bookweb.org.

American Library Association. www.ala.org. Retrieved November 18, 2016. www.ala.org.

Ancestry ProGenealogists. www.progenealogists.com. Retrieved November 17, 2016. www.progenealogists. com.

Association of Professional Genealogists. www.apgen. org. Retrieved November 19, 2016. www.apgen.org.

Autostraddle. www.autostraddle.com Retrieved November 18, 2016. www.autostraddle.com.

Clark, Dorie. "How To Make a Living From Blogging. " http://www.forbes.com/sites/dorieclark/2014/07/24/ how-to-make-a-living-from-blogging/#458474b027bc. Retrieved November 17, 2016Forbes. July 24, 2014. http://www.forbes.com/sites/dorieclark/2014/07/24/ how-to-make-a-living-from-blogging/#458474b027bc.

Duhaime's Law Dictionary. "Dictionary of Latin Legal Terms. " http://www.duhaime.org/LegalDictionary/Category/ LatinLawTermsDictionary.aspx. Retrieved November 18, 2016. http://www.duhaime.org/LegalDictionary/ Category/LatinLawTermsDictionary.aspx.

Kalsi, Loveish. "6 Tips For Becoming a Successful Blogger." http://www.shoutmeloud.com/6-tips-to-become-a-successful-blogger.html. Shout Me Load. Retrieved November 20, 2016. http://www.shoutmeloud.com/6-tips-to-become-a-successful-blogger.html.

The Law Society. "Alternative Careers." https://www.lawsociety.org.uk/careers/becoming-a-solicitor/alternative-careers/. Retrieved November 17, 2016. https://www.lawsociety.org.uk/careers/becoming-a-solicitor/alternative-careers/.

Media Bistro. www.mediabistro.com. Retrieved November 16, 2016. www.mediabistro.com.

National Archives. "Drafting Legal Documents."https://www.archives.gov/federal-register/write/legal-docs. Retrieved November 16. 2016. https://www.archives.gov/federal-register/write/legal-docs.

Necessary Trouble. www.necessarytrouble.org. Retrieved November 18, 2016. www.necessarytrouble.org.

Paz & Associates. www.pazbookbiz.com. Retrieved November 19, 2016. www.pazbookbiz.com.

Thompson, Clive. "A Timeline Of The History Of Blogging." New York Magazine, February 20, 2006. Web. Retrieved March 26, 2013.

Wortham, Jenna. "After 10 Years Of Blogs, The Future's Brighter Than Ever." Wired, December 17, 2007. Web. Retrieved March 26, 2013.

INDEX

ABOUT THE AUTHOR

Janelle Asselin is a writer and editor known for her work in comics.

Rebecca T. Klein has a BA in English from Marygrove College and an MA in English/secondary education from Brooklyn College. In addition to writing books for young adults, she nurtures their skills in reading, writing, and cultural analysis as a middle school English and social studies teacher in Detroit.

PHOTO CREDITS

Cover, p. 1 Jacob Lund/Shutterstock.com; pp. 4–5 dotshock/Shutterstock.com; p. 8 2p2play/Shutterstock.com; p. 10 Mario Tama/Getty Images; p. 13 Minerva Studio/Shutterstock.com; pp. 18–19 Jean-Christian Bourcart/Getty Images; pp. 20–21 Dasha Petrenko/Shutterstock.com; pp. 24–25 file404/Shutterstock.com; pp. 30–31 The Washington Post/Getty Images; pp. 34–35 GaudiLab/Shutterstock.com; pp. 36–37 Vitaliy Hrabar/Shutterstock.com; p. 44 Undrey/Shutterstock.com; pp. 46–47 Stephen Coburn/Shutterstock.com; pp. 54–55 Christian Science Monitor/Getty Images; pp. 58–59 IVY PHOTOS/Shutterstock.com; pp. 64–65 Nejron Photo/Shutterstock.com; p. 68 Orhan Cam/Shutterstock.com; pp. 70–71 Tyler Olson/Shutterstock.com; pp. 76–77 LiliGraphie/Shutterstock.com; pp. 82–83 © AP Images; pp. 84–85 Vladimir Volodin/Shutterstock.com; pp. 90–91 Kzenon/Shutterstock.com; pp. 96–97 antoniodiaz/Shutterstock.com; pp. 100–101 Pambrun Helene/Paris Match Archive/Getty Images; pp. 104–105 Rishiken/Shutterstock.com; pp. 110–111 WAYHOME studio/Shutterstock.com; pp. 114–115 KP Photograph/Shutterstock.com; cover and interior design elements © iStockphoto.com/David Shultz (dots), Melamory/Shutterstock.com (hexagon pattern), Lost & Taken (boxed text background texture), bioraven/Shutterstock.com (chapter opener pages icons).

Designer: Brian Garvey; Editor and Photo Researcher: Bethany Bryan